Grandparenting:

Tales from the Crib

When Your Children Become Parents

Dr. Stephanie Kutzen

Global Source Publishing, Inc.

Chicago

Published by
Global Source Publishing, Inc.
405 N. Oak, Mount Prospect, Illinois.

Design and layout
Stephanie Shinkarev
Global Source Publishing, Inc.

Library of Congress Control Number: 2006926920

ISBN: 0-9786012-0-3

First Edition

Printed in Moldova

A Legacy of Laughter

Dedication

This book is dedicated to my mother, Annette Grace, and to my father, Moray Kutzen, for encouraging me to learn, live and love; and to my children, Beth, Joel, and his wife, Amy.
Lovingly in my corner, you all bring joy to this accomplishment.

Acknowledgements

My magnificent friends and colleagues, whose personal gifts encourage my endeavors: Susan Primer, Monica Fernandez, Armand Oliva, Ellen Goldsmith, Adar Rathe, Leighton and Mary Clark, Larry Weinstein, Rabbi Douglas and Peggy Goldhammer, Cindy Beranek, Hashem J. Haleem, Muriel Goodfriend, Ellie Berkson, Yvette Freedberg, Evelyn Grossman, and the late Judith Weinstein.

Grandparenting:

Tales from the Crib

When Your Children Become Parents

A Legacy of Laughter

Stephanie Kutzen, Ph.D.

hmmm humm ♪ ♪♪

Table of Contents

Limbo

In 2001, I found myself in a prickly place. I was 56 and uncharacteristically experiencing feelings of being in a no-woman's land. For more than three decades, my career in counseling, organizational consulting, and university teaching had been a source of affirmation and reward. But my mind and spirit were restless. I was itching for more diverse career challenges and my personal life was in flux after divorce. Looking over my life, I realized that despite all the bonuses and pleasures that had come with my various roles, my most enduring and loving accomplishment was as mother to son Joel and daughter Beth. Still, in truth, I sometimes found it difficult adjusting to my new role with them: as a parent to adult children. Was I to be a friend, an advisor, a protector, a provider of financial aid in a pinch, or all of the above?

Suddenly and strikingly, I found myself in a state of limbo – as a professional, as a partner and even more puzzlingly, as a parent.

Authors Bloomfield, Colgrove, and McWilliams (1991) describe *limbo* in their book *How to Survive the Loss of a Love*. To my astonishment, I saw a perfect mirror of myself on page 3. I was feeling a sense of loss related to aging and uncertainty. Are things on? Are they off? Is change a gain? Or is it a loss?

By nature and training, I am a problem solver. Moreover, I strongly believe in the principle that the good in your life comes by affecting your world to bring about positive outcomes. Yet I was struck by how difficult it was to generate solutions in this limbo state. I found myself, for once, neither here nor there.

Over the years, I have learned that if you sit still for awhile, life does change, issues are resolved or surprising developments may alter the current landscape. That summer, just such a turn of events took place. My son and his beautiful wife Amy announced their first baby was due in February: "*Mazel tov*! We're thrilled to make you a grandmother." My heart, soul, and entire body responded with great joy, but perhaps without the demure emotion befitting my new exalted role. I passed gas. The kids roared and my son remarked wryly that tears would have been fine too.

All at once, many of the perplexing issues in my professional and personal life shifted to a lower level of priority. At the kids' invitation, I dove into baby planning activities and their journey into parenthood with gusto. At the same time, I began my own renewal project; one that mattered more than I had ever dreamed would be possible. I became Grandma Mimi.

This book is about this new chapter in my life. It is intended to be a legacy of laughter: all the love and humor drawn from interacting with adult kids who are now, themselves, raising children.

Early on, I encountered other grandparents with their own treasure trove of anecdotes, adventures and observations – memories that enrich their families' lives, just as ours do. I began collecting these stories. By word of mouth, my project began to grow. My son, a high-tech guru, created a Web site (www.whenyourchildrenbecomeparents.com) so that I could solicit more stories from grandparents, aunts and uncles, godparents, and friends. The professorial side of Grandma Mimi became engaged and went to work. After months of research, I found a wide range of books and Web sites that speak to various aspects of grandparenting, including Billy Crystal's lovely book *I Already Know I Love You*. Published in 2004, it describes the comedian's feelings on becoming a grandfather for the first time. However, despite the diversity of offerings on the topic of grandparenting, I discovered a gap in the literature. There was nothing that highlighted the unique (and sometimes hilarious) interactions between parents and their adult children who have become parents.

My initial research included group questionnaires posted on the Web site, informal interviews, and presentations to local senior groups as well as my own growing list of funny stories recorded in my private journal. The feedback was overwhelmingly positive and resulted in an abundance of material from special and diverse contributors.

I would like to thank my children, Joel and Amy and Beth for giving me what I needed most for this project: a fan club that's always in my corner. Like me, they see this book and the humor that underlies it as a testament to the rich fabric of families and generational legacies.

My deep gratitude also goes to the contributors of the stories in this book. Some of you worried whether your kids would resent you for airing all their dirty diapers in public. Thanks to you and to them for sharing your insights and your laughter. Your submissions are pure gold and to be valued forever.

Chapter 1

Preparations and Strategies

The pregnancy was at the five-month mark when the kids called me about strategic *childcare planning*. This is a euphemism, I've learned, that thirty-something, two-income, yuppie couples use when they mean to say, "A baby? We're going to lose control of our freedom. "Help!" Both held rewarding careers that they wanted to keep—along with the baby. The childcare strategy that they outlined for me would accomplish both objectives. It included hiring a nanny for three days, having Amy home one day, and bringing me in every Friday. They explained how they wanted me to have a direct and strong influence on the baby's development. I immediately signed on to their plan and was overjoyed by the invitation. Later, I determined that I could maintain my income by working weekends and additional evenings. Just like that, my priorities shifted. My career became secondary to the important new job of being a link in our family legacy.

The new job requirements began to hit me squarely a few months before the delivery and amidst all the requisite shopping and baby room decorating. Joel called to explain that all *primary caregivers* (today's term for *babysitters*) were invited to attend an infant and child cardiopulmonary rescue (CPR) course at the local hospital. Early on, Amy's lovely mother Linda and I concluded this was not an invitation; it was commanded, on demand, and non-negotiable event. I saw it coming when Joel announced privately to me, "Mother, you have to pass this CPR class so you can baby sit." I left for class equipped with twenties in case I needed bribe money to pay off the instructors. Under the watchful eyes of my son, both grandmothers passed and were considered fit for emergency duty. I left class asking myself, "Since when did I have to prove anything to my kids?" Evidently, a rite of passage had begun. As a grandma to their children, my skills and limitations were forever fair game for their parental scrutiny. Whatever happened to my practical wisdom and experience? Both my son Joel and my daughter Beth survived into adulthood on my watch. Oh how the times were a changin'.

Then there was the shopping event at Babies-R-Us. Linda and I were cordially invited on a sunny Sunday to help outfit the upcoming arrivals: the baby, the nursing mother, the new father, and the nursery. Again, I was impressed by the kids' attentiveness to making the grandmothers feel welcome from the point of conception. Shopping began with Joel distributing a detailed spreadsheet, complete with aisle numbers. Joel quarterbacked assignments to ensure, according to him, an efficient, effective event. I flashbacked to 1970 and what had been a free-for-all shopping day with no list and much chaos preparing for Joel's arrival. At 24, I barely knew what a baby needed, let alone how to design a comprehensive list to ensure a baby's survival. Back in the moment, a new concern came to mind. Would Joel over-use his propensity to list and organize to manage his life as a parent? Certainly I can own up to a genetic contribution and a psychological model; as a proud Virgo, I demonstrated value in "keeping order" in our family life, but now Joel was showing me up, climbing over the top. Time would tell. I swallowed my concerns, checked my list, and moved down the aisle to the breast pumps.

Don't Stop the Parade for Baby!

In preparation for the birth of their first child, my daughter and son-in-law (both older than 38 years) developed a plan for my weeklong cross-country visit when the baby came. The plan for all of us included:

- Purchase coffee at Starbucks between 8 and 9 a.m. daily
- Rent videos from Blockbuster to watch every evening for entertainment
- Prepare a daily list and accomplish every item

The funny thing is that they really believed this was possible. The old saying still applies, "The best laid plans of mice and men have gone astray."

——Judy Levin, Leland, Michigan

Chapter 2

Birth Day Daze

My intent throughout this book, while conveying humor about my own and contributors' kids is to poke fun first at myself as I reminisce about how anxious I was as a first-time mom. A great illustration: my labor began around midnight on April 3, 1970. Although my water had clearly broken, I calmly said to my husband, "Don't bother taking my overnight bag. Must be false labor. I'm sure we won't be staying." Yikes! What planet was I from back then?

To my delight, my grandkid's birth was in progress. Joel asked me to go to Amy and offer moral support until he could get home from work. I stayed through the early stages of labor and left Joel with Amy to share a long night of preplanned birthing activities. This agenda had been designed in concert with their dula, a professional birthing partner. By then, I was acquainted with the who, what, and how of a dula's role throughout a pregnancy, in the delivery room, and upon the family's return home. Dulas are typically nurse practitioners trained as pre- and postnatal educators and coaches. The kids' dula advised them in the areas of nutrition, exercise, stress management, and their favorite, weekly massage therapy for the parents-to-be. This care builds to a crescendo when the dula assists the couple in the hospital delivery room. As a trio, they carry out prearranged activities to support a positive, nurturing structure that is meant to compliment, not interfere with ongoing medical procedures of the attending physicians and nurses.

As planned, Amy's mom Linda, the dula, and the kids went into the delivery room. I happily coordinated the waiting room social activities. A couple of hours later, the news was mixed. The good news: Amy's water had broken (all over her mom's shoes); the bad news: Amy's mom and the dula were facing off about whether Amy should keep wearing the birthing monitor. Amidst this tension, I acted upon the advice of a seasoned grandmother friend of mine. I began to hum. Humming is a terrific coping skill to add to your repertoire when you become a grandparent. Please try it.

With all differences aside, the arrival of Adina Joy Grossman rocked our world on February 22, 2002.

Tales from the Edge

The time had finally arrived. My daughter Kimi and her husband Ron called me to come to the hospital. Excited, I settled into the waiting area with my *machatootsies*, my pet word for Ron's parents. Seated near the birthing room, we heard Kimi's every groan, holler, grunt, and pitiful begging for more drugs to stop the pain. A few minutes later, Ron dashed out of the birthing room in a cold sweat, looking as white as a sheet, and asked, "Kimi is in so much pain. When will it stop?" His mother firmly told Ron to get his tail back into the room immediately. He went back in, and we had such a laugh. Finally, we heard the nurse tell Kimi to begin pushing. Always empathic with my daughter, I moved to a wall and started pushing in sync with the nurse's commands. Thank you, Lord. Baby Ronnie was born as my hemorrhoids started to dance.

——Harriet Goldberg, Glenview, Illinois

Check Those Toes

The minute I learned that my daughter Adar was pregnant, I was both ecstatic and fearful. I felt the thrill of having my first grandchild but at the same time I was anxious that the baby might inherit his grandfather's two webbed toes. Most people obsess about counting 10 fingers and 10 toes, but with our genetics at work, I imagined the worst. I started to drive my daughter batty with questions and comments. "Does the ultrasound show anything? Do you have any strange sensations in your uterus that the toes are webbed? If we're lucky the baby will be breech so we'll know right away."

When David was born, my daughter finally had her chance. When her dad and I arrived at the hospital, she told us that the pediatrician and nurses insisted that the baby be swaddled for 36 hours and, although she was sorry, she couldn't go against medical orders just to show us his feet. After what seemed like weeks (but was only an hour), Adar said, "Just kidding. Come look for yourself." With great relief, we saw two beautiful, normal feet. The moral of my funny story is that I guess genes don't necessarily make the man.

——Mrs. Lila Rossman, Los Angeles, California

Chapter 3

Infinite Infant Challenges

Many contributors sent me stories about how their kids, often unsure and anxious, turned into know-it-alls by living "by the book" with their first-borns. I can relate.

Contrary to the advice of some experts, I did not attend a preparatory course on how to be an effective, efficient, sensitive, stay-out-of-trouble grandparent. I chose instead to use common sense in approaching my new role. My first indication that the road into my kids' infant daze was going to be steep occurred when Adina was just 10 days old. I thoughtfully asked Joel how he and Amy wanted me to diaper the baby. After all, I explained, 34 years ago

I used cloth diapers and pins, and I wanted to do things their way as they used disposables. Off we went to the changing table for my lesson where Joel observed and critiqued my technique. Joel lovingly but tentatively, as new dads will do, positioned Adina on the table as a right-handed person. Well, as a lefty, I explained that I needed to turn her in the other direction to make it easier for me to diaper her. With deep conviction, Joel said these memorable words, "Mother, you can't turn Adina around to diaper her. She knows her head goes the other way." I grinned broadly at his funny, look-how-smart-my-newborn-is-already remark until he told me it was not a joke. He insisted that Adina would know the difference and that I should do my best to diaper her in a right-handed manner.

At 10 days old my first grandchild, according to her father, had reached an intellectual milestone. Folks, I stood in amazement at my son because he truly believed that he had birthed a child that possessed advanced cognitive development in the areas of problem solving, judgment, and decision-making. Oy!

Feeding Time

My first visit to see my infant granddaughter Robin continues to be one of my funniest memories. I vowed only to assist, not advise my daughter Phyllis who was toughing it out with a fussy baby. She had already told me that she was tense being observed by anyone, not just me, in carrying out new mom activities. Robin was crying nonstop when I arrived. In a loving way, I asked Phyllis when the baby last had a bottle. She said with deep conviction that Robin couldn't possibly be hungry because her last bottle was two hours and 15 minutes ago. "You see, Mother, my pediatrician gave me clear instructions to feed the baby every three-and-a-half hours or three at the earliest." I just hummed as she insisted on strictly following this schedule. My kid had to do things her way. Well, after enduring 30 more minutes of hunger cries, I looked at my daughter and said, "Show her the clock!"

——Minnie Chelnick, Chicago, Illinois

A Chemical Fallout

What a funny memory thinking back on when I visited my two-week-old godson for the first time. His dad, a chemist, proudly showed me the notebook for charting what the baby was going to do each day. He was convinced that by scientifically noting daily behaviors he could analyze the baby's performance and arrange a permanent schedule. Having raised four kids myself, imagine my surprise when the new dad called a week later confirming that the baby was unschedulable.

——Randy Williams, Palatine, Illinois

Assuming the Position

When my oldest daughter Dawn came home from the hospital with my grandson Lance, she stayed with us for the first week. Their first night home, the baby woke several times for a feeding. Dawn, blurry eyed and exhausted, would wake up and give him a bottle, and they would fall back to sleep. After a while, I heard the baby wake again, but this time he continued to cry for his bottle. I checked on Lance and found Dawn half-asleep next to the bassinet on her hands and knees crying in sync with the baby. It was a funny sight and sound. To this day, Dawn swears it never happened. I wish I owned a movie camera in those days.

——Lynda Norton, Bellwood, Illinois

What a Trip

As grandma's kindly do, I offered to baby sit when my son Gregg and his wife were sleep-deprived new parents. My grandson had severe colic and was a challenge. I arrived to find the kids with bags under their eyes deep enough to hold clothes for a week's vacation. While he paced, Gregg held Sean above his head, swinging the baby softly. When that technique no longer stopped the crying, Gregg put Sean on top of the running clothes dryer where they both vibrated off to sleep.

——Yvette Freedberg, Elk Grove Village, Illinois

Chapter 4

Lists That Do More Than Enumerate

By the time Joel and Amy felt they were ready to leave the baby for more simple errands, they agreed to attend a friend's wedding. At three months, Adina was now taking breast milk in a bottle and I could be trusted to manage all operations for an afternoon. It was terrific to see them dressing up and doing something novel like getting out and breathing some fresh air. I swear, there is a universal smell and look of a home with a new baby: from fresh flowers on dining room tables to mountains of Handi-wipes; from decorative floor vases to Diaper Genies. And instead of the sweet fragrance of perfume or cologne, the unforgettable smell of diaper ointments permeates the air.

It was on this day that a ritual was initiated that continues to affect my credibility. It is known as the transfer. Simply defined by Amy and Joel, it is the requisite time necessary to make a comfortable transition for the baby from the parents to another caregiver. This includes the actual handing over of the infant; updates on the last and next nap; the state of urinary and bowel conditions; instructions on how to heat and cool the house to keep the environment balanced; their cell, pediatrician, hospital, and poison control numbers; and, of course, a 30-second quiz on infant CPR procedures. The best was saved for last: the feeding schedule. Joel presented me with the following computer-generated list that remains among my precious mementos.

In case you are wondering, yes, I did alert Joel to my abilities in bottle feeding him and his sister. When the kids left for the wedding, I scratched my head wondering if all these years Joel imagined he was suckled by a wet nurse. I find myself in good company with other contributors, whose skills were judged "questionable".

Adina's Feeding Schedule: 12 noon—9 p.m.

1. Remove bottle from refrigerator
2. Wash hands
3. Put bottle in small bowl and place in sink
4. Don't forget to remove drain from sink to avoid flood
5. Turn on hot water to heat bottle in bowl
6. Be careful about temperature as breast milk damages
7. Rewash hands before giving bottle
8. Shake drops on wrist to ensure warm not hot
9. Begin, and remember to burp
10. Write down amount of bottle taken

Tantamount to Needing Oxygen

My sister and I were thrilled when asked to baby sit her six-month-old granddaughter Danielle for an entire day. We arrived promptly at 9 a.m., ready to play and have fun. Instead, we were greeted with a seven-page, single-spaced, typed list of instructions. We sat down and studied: Duckie had to be on the high chair or Danielle would not eat. The blue blanket was for napping. The yellow goes in the playpen. Pacifiers were to be boiled immediately if they hit the floor. Spoons of peas were to be tipped in applesauce or she would not eat them; carrots with apricot. It went on and on. After two hours of serious adherence to the list, we looked at each other and laughed. Between us, we had raised 10 children without a list. So we put Danielle on a blanket on the floor and she happily played while we settled in to watch Dr. Phil.

——Corinne Edwards, Chicago, Illinois

Directions included in the box

As a mother of four, I eagerly awaited the birth of my first grandchild. When my daughter-in-law and son asked me to baby sit my grandson for the first time, I arrived with great anticipation. The apprehensive new mother greeted me and immediately handed me two printed lists.   The first one detailed a dozen or so actions to take if the baby cried. The second list was a set of instructions on how to use a baby carriage to take the baby for a walk. I smiled to myself, pleased that I had managed to get my kids past infancy.

——Marlene Rabin, Wilmette, Illinois

GUIDE TO CARING FOR ADINA JOY GROSSMAN

BEDTIME

YOU SHOULD START GETTING HER READY FOR BED AROUND **6:45PM** AT THE LATEST. MAKE SURE TO BRING UP A SIPPY CUP OF WATER WITH YOU.

- PUT HER ON THE CHANGING TABLE; CHANGER HER DIAPER; LUBE HER UP WITH THE UNPETROLEUM JELLY.
- PUT ON HER PAJAMAS. (SHE LIKES TO PICK.)
- TURN THE **NIGHTLIGHT** ON NEXT TO HER CRIB.
- **CLOSE ALL THE SHADES** AND TURN OUT ALL THE LIGHTS, EXCEPT THE LAMP NEXT TO THE GLIDER CHAIR.
- CHECK THE **HEATER** TEMPERATURE. ON **COOL NIGHTS**, WE KEEP IT SET BETWEEN "2" AND "3". (THAT'S THE SETTING ON THE MACHINE, NOT THE ACTUAL TEMP.) ON **WARM NIGHTS**, 2 IS FINE.
- AFTER YOU HAVE READ HER 3 STORIES, PRESS PLAY ON THE **CD PLAYER** UNDER HER CRIB.
- OFFER HER MORE WATER.
- TURN OUT THE LIGHT AND SAY, "WE'RE HAVING A TALK."
- WHEN SHE'S DONE, "FLY" HER INTO THE CRIB.
- PLAY SHADOWNS ON THE WALL AND SING.
- **COUNT 1-2-3, THEN TURN OFF THE NIGHTLIGHT.**
- SHE WILL SLEEP. MAYBE SHE'LL MAKE A LITTLE NOISE FOR AWHILE, BUT THEN SHE'LL SLEEP.

GO DOWNSTAIRS. TURN THE MONITOR ON.

SHE MAY MAKE RANDOM NOISES AND SHORT CRIES THROUGHOUT THE NIGHT.
THIS IS NORMAL.

PLUG IN THE MONITOR NEXT TO THE BED WHERE YOU WILL SLEEP. THE MONITOR MUST BE PLUGGED IN ORDER TO WORK.

Chapter 5

Medical Mania

As I prepared to outline this chapter, I reread my own journal accounts of first first-aid stories. Although I didn't find the following account funny, I do believe it reflects the goodness of Joel and Amy that outshines what I call their *unique parenting nuances*. This incident marked the first time Adina was injured on my watch. She was, at that time, two-and-a-half years old.

Using Your Noggin

Today was Friday, Grandma's day, marked by a mix of pleasure and pain. The day was summer beautiful with a visit to our local botanical gardens on the morning agenda. It was just us girls. New baby brother Joshua stayed at home with Amy. With the exception of Adina occasionally plucking a rare species of rose for mommy, it was an exceptional day. Then it happened: Adina's first big fall on a gravel sidewalk with me standing behind her. The result was a big bloody scrape and a bump on the back of her head. Without much drama, the boo-boo was medically managed and we returned to our day of fun.

Later, at home with Adina napping, Joel and Amy really were there for me when I had a delayed reaction to this precious child getting hurt. As I neared tears, they consoled and reminded me that kids are built to fall and they spring back. They pointed out that I cannot carry around Adina and Joshua until they are 18, even if I want to protect them. Their compassion and lightness of being reminded me once again what great people they are to have as parents of my grandchildren.

——Grandma Mimi, Journal entry of August 6, 2004

Teeth or Consequences

I was babysitting for my nine-month-old grandson, which had become my best job after retiring as a fireman. Max Jr. somehow squirmed his way out of my arms and, to my horror, his front tooth was chipped as his mouth hit the glass table. I rushed the baby to the hospital all the while mortified that he would never look right and I would never be trusted again by my son and daughter-in-law to baby sit. When the kids arrived and the doctor began attending to Max, I was in such a state of high anxiety that they gently suggested I go home. Later that evening, the pediatrician called me at home to say, "The baby is fine, but it's you I'm worried about." Max Jr. is now a strapping teenager and we still laugh about the day that Grandpa was treated by his baby doctor.

——Max Grovenor, Evanston, Illinois

What? An Emergency?

I was so proud when my son James and his partner Lyle adopted their baby and entered fatherhood for the first time. Their happiness enlivened our whole family as we participated in Mai's bonding. However, when she became ill for the first time under their care, a classic story was born.

As the local grandma, I vowed to advise only when asked. Things were beyond advice the day I walked into their house and heard my frantic son on the phone repeating to their pediatrician's answering service, "My daughter isn't breathing. What should I do?" Stunned but quick on my feet, I told Lyle to call

911 and start infant CPR. A pregnant pause came over the room when they stopped me and announced that the medical emergency was Mai's very stuffy nose.

I am pleased to report that dads and daughter are doing quite well after many months on the firing line. I still chuckle when I remember James' and Lyle's response to the baby's first cold.

——Mrs. Gerri Solomon, Denver, Colorado

Joel's Nose Knows

As a toddler, my son Joel perceived the good, the bad, the tasty, and the yucky of life through a strong sense of smell. His food preferences to this day reflect the smell-first-and-then-eat strategy. Guess it isn't a big surprise that Joel has proven to be one of the world's best dads at sniffing out dangers to his little family. For example, a dear friend joined 18-month-old Adina and me for a lunch visit when I was babysitting. I heated three cheese-and-broccoli-stuffed baked potatoes in the microwave. The aroma hung pleasantly in the kitchen as we enjoyed our visit and lunch. The kids' arrived home from work and I left for the day, reveling in Adina's antics. Moments later, Joel called my cell and whined, "MOTHER! Why does our microwave smell like throw-up? Was Adina sick and you just didn't want to tell us she vomited when you were here?"

I couldn't let this one pass. Sure, veggie-cheese spuds were the culprit, but why not give my kid a little back. I recounted "the story": Adina had been so naughty that I punished her by putting her in the microwave and setting it on high, and she threw up. I asked if he approved of my disciplinary measures. He smelled a rat so I told him the true, cheesy story. He lightened up as I assured him that somewhere in the universe his behavior is considered very normal. No matter what, I love watching Joel as a dad, even when he is a stinker.

——Grandma Mimi, Journal entry of August 12, 2003

Chapter 6

CSI: Crime and Silly Investigations

The tides turned in my grandma role one Friday when my frustration peaked to meet Joel's anxiety levels in caring for his infant daughter. Although the incident is humorous in hindsight, at the time I was incredulous about my son's critical behavior. This story and the accompanying submissions could certainly be considered as a new plot direction for the popular television series Crime Scene Investigation (CSI).

Adina was just a bit of a thing, maybe two months old, when after a feeding she spit up some milk on the changing table as I changed her diaper. I remember thinking how my own kids, especially

Beth, mastered the art of projectile spitting. How amazing to see the cycle of human growth and development in my granddaughter without having to wear washables every day until she drinks from a cup. As I daydreamed, I used a cloth diaper to adeptly clean up the wet milk on the pad and, *voila*, all was fine in our world. Or so I thought.

The kids returned early to relieve me and to visit with out-of-town guests who were staying at their house. As I packed my belongings to leave, Joel asked me to go upstairs with him for a minute because he wanted to show me something. To Adina's room we went, and once there Joel held up the pink pad from her changing table. The inquisition began. "Motherrrrr, why is this pad wet? It smells." I explained how the baby's spit up had just dampened the pad and it was no big deal. Joel lapsed into a tirade about how he and Amy had to know absolutely everything that transpired during their absence and that I must document, not hide, incidents like these that could well be health forecasters. I gave him my most steely look and retorted, "What is this? A crime scene investigation?"

Back at my home, I phoned Joel and informed him that he had crossed the line in the manner in which he corrected his now "hot mama." Joel apologized, I accepted, and I agreed to write up the events that occurred on my Fridays with Adina. The lesson I came away with: hide the evidence. I never left their house again without disposing of everything incriminating. I washed all soiled pad covers, stained blankets, and tell-tale signs of trouble on baby clothes, crib sheets, and the high chair. I smirk with pleasure while informing you that I was never caught or convicted of another crime. Case closed.

London Bridges

I have made many interesting and often humorous observations about my daughter since she became a parent. Plenty of opportunities arise because I care for my grandson Cole two days a week at my home while his mom works. But there's a distinctly different reaction between events that occur at my home and those that occur at my daughter's. For instance, if Cole gets a boo-boo at his house, his parents respond calmly; it's no big deal. But if a bit of an accident happens on my watch, I get the third degree as if I am a crook under the hot lights.

One time I just had to give it back when my daughter, in her most accusing voice questioned, "And just how did my son get that scrape on his knee? Where were you when that happened? Why weren't you watching?" I answered, "I was watching. I watched him fall down."

——Myrna Smith, Skokie, Illinois

Quality Control Level

I have wiped, washed, and whisked off pee and poop from my great nieces and nephews for the last five years, thank you. But my niece Julie and her partner Gayle have topped all of my babysitting stories to date. They were recovering well from nervous moms disorder. At least that's what I thought. I had just finished changing my great niece Rachel, fluffing and buffing her with all the requisite wipes and creams. In came her moms and I watched in amazement as they unlatched her diaper for a quality control check. I turned to them and said, "Guess it's time for my weekly performance review." They laughed. I sighed.

——Sally Kelley, Spokane, Washington

A No-fault Reconciliation

Our son and his wife invited us over recently to have the honor of giving our grandson his first bath. Thrilled, we arrived at our kids' request only to find that before we could proceed we were expected to watch a video on a new method for bathing an infant. We casually asked what could possibly be new under the sun about baths. They explained that today's "experts" recommend infants be placed in the bath water while completely dressed and, once in the water, the baby should be undressed one piece of

clothing at a time. As seasoned grandparents, we had patiently dealt with the how-to lists and tedious instructions of our other three kids as they became parents. Remaining calm, we said that we preferred bathing the baby in the traditional way rather than watching the video. Their response still has us reeling: "No video, no bath." This led to a first. Instead of the baby, the grandparents were thrown out with the bathwater.

——Loving (traditional) grandparents

Chapter 7

Act II

For 13 months, or approximately 55 Fridays, I had the time of my life caring for Adina Joy. I became her muse, dancing the rumba or reading to coax last bites down. Traditions developed like "Friday is grandma day, and that means ice cream day." By then, I had taught Adina how to crack and scramble an egg and to mush and enjoy ice cream after every lunch together. I chanted *bravo* when she finished the lines of the silly songs I sang to her. One special one has passed through four generations of our family: "Hi, hi, hi. Me got a skillio, make like a skallio, punch in eye" became a favorite. Later on, "Happy Talk" from the classic show *South Pacific* was on our top 10. I introduced Adina to Mickey D's and we became the ladies that lunch at local spots. Not a Friday went by that I didn't fall more in love with my grandchild, not for her beauty, her verbal aptitude, or charm. Rather, I found Adina reflecting my love and adoration for her back to me in a mirror image. I realized I had not felt this pure, almost piercing experience since I was a young girl with my own babies. This part of the legacy is significant as the hours of our lives may not often be touched with such remarkable moments of unconditional love. But, let me tell you, I began to crave for more of them.

It is rare that you get just what you ask for, but news of the kids' second pregnancy renewed my belief that everything is possible. Hopes high, our families were thrilled to add more to the legacy of family growth and continuity. However, the second act opened with my daughter-in-law experiencing morning sickness that morphed into day and night sickness and lasted until the baby's birth. Amy, with Joel's undivided support, held on with full-time nausea, a full-time job, and a toddler to raise for nine gritty months. Amy's family, the Schiffmans, were very supportive under the loving and fine leadership of her mom Linda. Together, with the kind and generous support of my daughter Beth, we offered respite care one evening a week, namely to care for Adina and do what was needed in their house. The tradition born from this second act, "Tuesday nights with Grandma Mimi," exists even today.

According to Amy, my most special contribution to her was preparing fresh, homemade mashed potatoes. In her first trimester, her only sustenance was protein bars, bottled water, and prenatal vitamins when she could hold them down. One day she mentioned that she had a taste for mashed potatoes so I whipped up my mother's famous recipe. The poor kid was in heaven to be able to tolerate something she loved; it became my pleasure to ensure a full six-month supply. But the best memories of this time revolve around binding the ties with the kids and imprinting with Adina. I felt movement away from the no-woman's land to a more defined, comfortable role with my adult kids and the sheer joy of being childlike in play with Adina. I began to retool and refresh some tired aspects of my consulting business. My lovely daughter Beth, like a wished for gift, returned to live in Chicago after some years in California. Life was better now that she was with us to make the memories fuller. She and Adina began a unique aunt/niece connectedness. I was content to await Act II, the baby that would layer even more color and texture onto our family tree.

While I waited, I began to notice differences in the ways the kids prepared for a second child. The most obvious was the lack of how-to pregnancy literature. I anticipated the transformation of their den into an elaborate second baby room, exquisitely furnished like Adina's, a la baby Pottery Barn. Her yellow room was ready for occupancy months before arrival but that just wasn't happening this time. Near the due date I inquired, just once, how the den would be set up with the crib. The kids casually said the furniture would come "some time." Well, the crib did arrive and it became the only official evidence that a second child was to live in the den. No artfully planned infant décor seemed necessary to these veteran parents, not even a new coat of paint. I wasn't asked to tag along on another baby shopping expedition, but I did notice an extra diaper-changing pad waiting for use in the den closet. These were welcome signs of the well-known, second-child syndrome called "relax, we figured it out already."

Wonderful Joshua Moray Grossman was born on March 24, 2004, the next shining link to our family circle. I'm pleased to say that his arrival only minimally burst the bubble of his parent's "comme ci, comme ça" approach as they turned their attention to blending two-year-old, queen bee Adina with new-on-the-block brother. Like them, I found myself going around another bend, giving my love and energy to bonding with my new grandson while holding on to the powerful and rare singularity of my union with my granddaughter. Even more challenging was my task in taking care of two kids at one time, both requiring eyes, ears, and hands full time. Well, I grew into the job and after the first month figured out how to feed, burp, and soothe Joshua while doing the hokey-pokey with Adina and her dancing Elmo doll.

My curiosity was piqued even more when I came to realize that Joshua's changing pad was never to be attached to a changing table in his room but was stationed on the dining room table for convenience. The seeds of Joshua as the adaptive, go-with-the-flow, second child seemed to start here.

I had a hunch that other interesting nuances developed as siblings came into the family mix. The next stories and observations turned my hunch into reliable and valid grandparent truths.

The 10-Second Rule

We love the joy of being the grandma and grandpa of a granddaughter and now a grandson. Parenting a second child seems to have finally brought our kids back to normal. Instead of worrying and stressing over every little hygienic detail, they have adopted what they call *the 10-second rule*. This means if whatever falls on the floor or ground hasn't been there for more than 10 seconds, the baby can put it back in his mouth. What growth!

——Phyllis and Ben Kaplan, Highland Park, Illinois

Over the Top

During my daughter's first pregnancy, she constantly worried that I would overfeed, overdress, and overprotect her son. She even made a rule that I could only take care of the baby a few times a week. When grandson Nicolas arrived, she seemed to have a new attitude to match the added work in taking care of two kids. I remember how she came to me exhausted and pleaded, "Take them all you want. Overfeed, overdress, overprotect, but just take over!"

——Svetlana Kaminsky, Kiev, Ukraine

Second Time Around

One Saturday night, our son Jeff and his wife
Dana had a party at their home, inviting other
couples like themselves with little ones who seldom
had an evening out. As usual, we were thrilled when
asked to baby sit for our grandchildren and came
over to their house. Grandpa Joe rallied the troops;
five-year old twins Sam and David had baths, books,

68

bananas and bedtime snuggles. Three year old Rose had been asleep but woke up wailing a few hours later. Jeff and Dana told us to bring her down to join the party, figuring it would stop the tears and tire her. The visiting princess was the hit of the party as she wandered around visiting her many admirers. With our children in charge we went off duty and mingled with the guests.

It was 9 pm and Rosie was dancing and by 10 pm she was singing; as grandparents we were amazed knowing that her brothers, the princes, could never gotten away with this. By 11pm she was noshing but at the stroke of midnight, our princess finally turned into Sleeping Beauty.

——Mr. And Mrs. Sam Lerner, Hollywood, California

Chapter 8

Identity Theft

The juggling necessary to balance professional, personal, and grandparenting roles can be an art. Years in the counseling field have taught me that keeping clear boundaries and identities help when you change hats often. I was Dr. Kutzen in the academic-consulting world; Stephanie with friends and colleagues; Mom to my kids; and Grandma Mimi to toddler Adina and baby Joshua. My appointment book and my identities were joining nicely in a handshake. Or so I thought. Over the span of a few months, I began to note a gradual transformation.

Notes and invitations sent by the kids began coming, addressed to Grandma Mimi or Grandma

Kutzen. Rarely did anyone in the family call me by my name or even the title I held for 35 years: Mom. My name was being changed to reflect the newer and more comprehensive me, the grandma. I don't remember ever being consulted about a title change but intuitively understood that I was elevated up the family ladder to a wisdom position.

My approach to the shift was to keep light, stay sharp, and capture the ongoing humor that I and other grandparents have found in the everyday parenting stories about our kids. The stories in this chapter reflect the multiple layers we find in life transitions: laughter, joy, change, loss, hope, and continuity.

Growing up, my mother told me that a person sees himself or herself as old when they only wear sensible shoes. Into my 50s, I began to knock off a few inches from my high heels but still preferred wearing beautiful, youthful shoes. This came to mind when Joel and I had a discussion about another one of my more youthful indulgences: sports cars. I chuckled at how his recommendation for selecting my new car differed from his adolescence now that he was a dad. It was clearly influenced by my identity change and based on sensible grandma criteria. First some history.

When Joel first started driving, he was a hot shot driving my car, a black Pontiac Trans Am convertible. He was a kid with a fast car and the speeding tickets to prove it. He eventually settled down when he came to realize that tickets meant fines, court dates, and begging parents for loans that required repayment. I, however, maintained my penchant for sports cars and by 1996 had nicely matured by owning a high-power, two-door convertible import.

I loved my car, but it wasn't one to be used when the grandkids arrived. No sweat. I mastered driving the family SUV to outings and activities. Shortly after Joshua's birth in 2004, I mentioned to Joel that I was shopping for a car due to major repair costs common in older models. Joel's response immediately framed the purchase in terms of my identity progression from individual to his children's grandmother: "Mom, I think you should seriously consider buying a more sensible car this time, one with four doors so our kids can ride in it, too. It can still be stylish. If you do that, I'll even buy you two car seats."

Wow! Hearing this made me pause in thought. According to my son, this grandma thing had become the central reference point in my life. Exploring my aging issues became relevant. I pondered over the issue briefly. I decided that my next car would not be roomy or average looking with two car seats for chauffeuring the grandkids. For sure, no sensible shoes for me either. At least, not yet!

Some contributors' stories center on their kids adjusting to post-delivery body changes and altered lifestyles. Other poignant stories tell of how the birth of grandchildren brings change yet, at the same time, further cements family legacies.

Altered State

I was lucky to spend a month with my daughter Tami and son-in-law Chad when my granddaughter Hannah was born two years ago. I've enjoyed many proud moments because of Tami's numerous life accomplishments. Another great moment was when she became a mom and dealt with some changes just like a champ.

The kids live in Boulder, Colorado, where they enjoy outdoor sports and activities like hiking, riding, and camping. According to Tami, Chad and most of their friends are very involved in competitive physical sports, like mountain biking, marathons, and skiing. When Hannah was about a month old, we attended a party with Tami and Chad's friends. I swear, they were the most physically fit human beings I have ever seen. Tami, already bummed that her body was looking less buff, whispered her concerns in my ear. We smiled knowingly together as people around the room discussed the Tour de France, their recent triathlon accomplishments, and the number of miles they ran uphill daily. But my girl, never one to lose her confidence or wit, stood up and said proudly, "But I made it through 15 hours of labor with no epidural. So there."

——A Proud Mom

A Mere Reflection

When my daughter Becky was expecting her first child, we began to compare notes about our pregnancies. We soon recognized this shared experience was reshaping our identities by adding a *compadre* dimension to our parent-child relationship. At one point, I said to Becky, "You are not going to believe how much you are going to love your baby. It will hit you out of the blue and actually bring you to your knees." Becky said she could not imagine feeling so strongly about anything.

A few months after baby Stella arrived, Becky called me in tears one morning and said, "Oh Mom, it happened. I can't believe how much I love my little girl. And even though I never thought to tell you this before I became a mom myself, I want you to know how sorry I am about that time in college when I went to Turkey for three weeks and never called home once."

——Carol Stone, Crystal Lake, Illinois

Chapter 9

The Legacy

I hope you have enjoyed the stories and experiences describing the journey many of us take when our children become parents. However, I must admit, as other contributors have, that there are times—past and present—when we probably should have had our heads examined for quietly tolerating our kids' more annoying parenting quirks.

However, from day one, I wanted a grandparenting plan that would allow me to work well with my kids. It was built around good communication, being available emotionally and physically, and perfecting the art of humming to best manage quirks—theirs and mine. Now, as I evaluate the plan almost 1,460 days later, I claim it as a success. Common sense tells me not to mess with a good thing. Grandma Mimi is fortunate and happy to have her own key to Joel, Amy, Adina, and Joshua's home, and most importantly, their hearts. As the stories throughout this book reflect, it is only natural and human to encounter some bumps in the transition from parenting to grandparenting. I believe with conviction that hard work smoothes out the bumps and ensures the likelihood of more firmly knotted family ties with our next generations.

Family legacies teem with funny stories and memories full of poignancy and life lessons. Consider documenting your family's history through stories and purposefully passing them along as a gift to your descendents. Legacies bring us a small measure of immortality and don't leave our kids with any tax consequences.

I try every day in some way to think about the emotional and spiritual gifts I receive from my kids and grandchildren. I did so today when there was a bump to be noted and filed away for posterity.

Arriving a mere 10 minutes late to baby sit, Joel anxiously greeted me with, "Mother, when you're late, you bring tension to our whole family." Sure, I could have reacted and demanded a salve of appreciation for my contributions or pointed out his distorted thinking. Instead, I opted to think of my most recent gift: the toast Amy and Joel composed and read on the occasion of my 60th birthday.

A toast to our mother, an incredible woman to be sure. One who has devoted herself to our children with trips for ice cream, the library, and even manicures. She's been with them every Friday since they were born and Tuesday nights for dinner. Without her they'd be forlorn. For she's their Grandma Mimi, their playmate, caregiver, and teacher. She showers them with love. So compassionate and full of zest. Just a

few of her best features. There's nothing
she wouldn't do for us and this is not
just something she's said. During our
summer vacation in Michigan, for Adina
and Joshua, she gave up her bed. But
her love for us goes deeper than just her
devotion to the kids. She has been a
wonderful friend and mother and on our
happiness she's insisted. Steph gives
herself so completely to a special project,
person, or cause. And when tough times
roll her way, she hardly gives them a
pause. So on this day, your 60th, we
wish you great joy, all the good things in
life. Thank you for helping us to be a
better father, husband, mother, and
wife. Your friendship means the world to
us. Your support is never ending. You
just keep getting better. So a toast
l'chaim, to life, we are sending.

You can be sure, Grandma Mimi will always keep coming back on Fridays, Tuesdays, and when needed. This journey is not just mine but my descendents. I wish it to be repeated by my children and their children and their children...

A Note to My Children

This legacy of laughter began long before you, Joel, became a parent. It started with me, a 24-year-old, inexperienced new mother, lacking in common sense and scared silly. I worked with what I did have to make up for my limitations. And just what did I have? My great love for you and your sister Beth, a worn copy of Dr. Spock, and a great will to raise you both to bring honor to yourselves. I had egg on my face so many times but learned that poking fun at myself made for great family stories that you both enjoyed hearing as you were growing up. As adults, I know you still love this classic.

Your pediatrician, Joel, advised that at six months, babies should be fed pureed proteins, including egg yolks, which came in glass jars back in 1970. I followed the medical advice to a T and, fearing the "or else" possibilities, did everything I was told. One day I called Dr. Scheinberg in a state of high anxiety. I had run out of jars of egg yolks! After a long pause Dr. Scheinberg said, "Take it easy. Boil some eggs and give him the yolks." Deeply embarrassed, I mumbled something stupid like, "Why didn't I think of that?"

To you, Joel, Amy and Beth, I take full responsibility for setting the original standard in making mistakes as a new parent. As a result, my book is not a critique of your or others' parenting style but an effort to find the humor in the common challenges we all face when we become parents.

Thanks for the memories. Promise me, on our love, to keep the threads of these stories of laughter so they become the legacy you give to your children, and they to their children, and on and on.

Special Thanks

My special thanks to all the contributors who shared personal stories, anecdotes and memories via my Web site (www.whenyourchildrenbecomeparents.com), questionnaires, lectures and presentations. Please note that those wishing to be named in the book have given their legal waiver, while names and locations of others have been changed to protect their privacy.

And special thanks to:

- ✓ My sister, Judy Levin, for being my first and best cheerleader.
- ✓ My nieces and nephews, Stephen and Lisa Schwartz and Lisa and Jerry Jewel who always support Auntie.
- ✓ My dear friends and relatives, who offered ideas and material, especially Adar Rathe for her creative, humorous additions to the manuscript and for reading it "one more time".
- ✓ Carol Brockman, whose skillful editing provided the necessary polish and pizzazz.
- ✓ Global Source Publishing, Inc.'s Danice Kern and Marat Shinkarev for their exuberance, expertise and strong belief in a first-time, regional writer.
- ✓ Stephanie Shinkarev for using her artistic gifts to create this book's graphic illustrations.
- ✓ Author Gail Reichlin for her generous time and wisdom as a coach.
- ✓ Michael Manley for his guidance into the literary world.
- ✓ Roger Stein for his expert legal advice.